Corny Names & Stupid Places

SIDNEY S. PRASAD

DEDICATION

I dedicate this book to my good friend Manu. If you ever end up teaching a geography class, maybe you can touch on one of the destinations in this book!

CONTENTS

ACKNOWLEDGMENTS

Have you ever caught yourself off guard and got yourself startled by a mere street sign? You swear you were day dreaming because the sign was way too profound. All of a sudden you become infatuated with confirming this mirage and drive back. Sure enough your eyes didn't deceive you. The first thing you do is laugh and then you want to tell the whole world about your shocking discovery.

When you get home you make a couple of calls and tell your family and friends about your little field trip. With amazement you find out there are even more cheesy names and bizarre places in existence. Everybody all of a sudden starts talking about the corkiest places that they have visited. Now you have successfully started a game where all of you are on the hunt to top off the last sign.

I thought I would make it easier for you and open up my vault. I have travelled all over the world and have been exposed to some outrageously funny street signs. Please allow me to entertain and mesmerize you with a list of Corny Names and Stupid Places!

1 STUPID STREET SIGNS

LICKMAN ROAD, CHILLIWACK, CANADA

KATIE CROTCH ROAD, EMBDEN, UNITED STATES

HARDON ROAD, WOLVERHAMPTON, ENGLAND

DICKS ROAD, ROCKINGHAM, UNITED STATES

PE'E ROAD, POIPU, UNITED STATES

HARRY DICK ROAD, DOUGLAS, CANADA

MIANUS ROAD, STAMFORD, UNITED STATES

TITMAN ROAD, FAIRY BOWER, AUSTRALIA

BALD KNOB ROAD, BALD KNOB, AUSTRALIA

ASS ROAD, IBHAYI, SOUTH AFRICA

SEAMAN AVENUE, NEW YORK, UNITED STATES

FEARLESS AVENUE, LYNN, UNITED STATES

DOG FISH AVENUE, KALIFORNSKY, UNITED STATES

DUTCH OVEN AVENUE, SALEM, UNITED STATES

ELECTRIC AVENUE, BELLINGHAM, UNITED STATES

SEXTANS AVENUE, OCEAN SHORES, UNITED STATES

STONER AVENUE, SHREVEPORT, UNITED STATES

CRETIN AVENUE, SAINT PAUL, UNITED STATES

MULDER AVENUE, OTTAWA, CANADA

DE COCK AVENUE, CAPE TOWN, SOUTH AFRICA

BUTTHOLE LANE, SHEPSHED, ENGLAND

SLUTSHOLE LANE, NORFOLK, ENGLAND

DUMB WOMAN'S LANE, RYE, ENGLAND

COCKSHUT LANE, LANGWITH, ENGLAND

CROOKED LANE, DALLAS, UNITED STATES

SANTA CLAUS LANE, NEW CASTLE, UNITED STATES

I DREAM OF JEANNIE LANE, COCOA BEACH, UNITED STATES

FANNY HANDS LANE, LUDFORD, ENGLAND

CORNY NAMES & STUPID PLACES

HAG LANE, HALIFAX, ENGLAND

MIRACLE LANE, MISHAWAKA, UNITED STATES

LOIS LANE, HARRISONBURG, UNITED STATES

HILLBILLY LANE, AUSTIN, UNITED STATES

LONG LOVER LANE, HALIFAX, ENGLAND

UNEXPECTED ROAD, BUENA, UNITED STATES

STANDARD ROAD, HOUNSLOW, ENGLAND

RAW DYKES ROAD, LEICESTER, ENGLAND

CEMETERY ROAD, BRADFORD, ENGLAND

SELDOM SEEN ROAD, BRADFORD WOODS, UNITED STATES

SEXSMITH ROAD, RICHMOND, CANADA

HORNE ROAD, SOOKE, CANADA

SHORT CUT ROAD, RALEIGH, AUSTRALIA

OLD GUY ROAD, DAMON, UNITED STATES

MORNINGWOOD DRIVE, SAN MARCOS, UNITED STATES

BIZARRE DRIVE, NEW CASTLE, UNITED STATES

BONERWOOD DRIVE, NASHVILLE, UNITED STATES

CLITHERO DRIVE, BOISE, UNITED STATES

DICKINBEN DRIVE, SUMMERFIELD, UNITED STATES

POOH DRIVE, ALLENHURST, UNITED STATES

SUICIDE DRIVE, PAULDEN, UNITED STATES

BALLS HEAD DRIVE, WAVERTON, AUSTRALIA

COCKSHUTT ROAD, PORT DOVER, CANADA

NO NAME ROAD, LOOMIS, UNITED STATES

ZZYZX ROAD, SAN BERNARDINO, UNITED STATES

GEECK ROAD, DURAND, UNITED STATES

AAAA ROAD, HOWARD SPRINGS, AUSTRALIA

CANNIBAL ROAD, LOLETA, UNITED STATES

FAIL ROAD, SNOHOMISH, UNITED STATES

HI LO BIDDY ROAD, PUTNEY, UNITED STATES

THIS AIN'T IT ROAD, DADEVILLE, UNITED STATES

CORNY NAMES & STUPID PLACES

FARFROMPOOPEN ROAD, STORY, UNITED STATES

CUMMINGTON STREET, BOSTON, UNITED STATES

DILDO STREET, LEWISPORTE, CANADA

WALL STREET, NEW YORK, UNITED STATES

NO NAME ROAD, LONDONDERRY, UNITED STATES

WHY STREET, PRETORIA, SOUTH AFRICA

AWESOME STREET, CARY, UNITED STATES

GAY STREET, PHOENIXVILLE, UNITED STATES

BONER STREET, NEWARK, UNITED STATES

KNIGHTRIDER STREET, LONDON, ENGLAND

COCKBURN STREET, CAMBRIDGE, ENGLAND

MAYBE STREET, BOMBALA, AUSTRALIA

VIRGIN STREET, MONTEREY, UNITED STATES

BAD GEORGE ROAD, SUGARLOAF KEY, UNITED STATES

MAD BOB ROAD, SUMMERLAND KEY, UNITED STATES

ROCKY ROAD, SUGARLOAF KEY, UNITED STATES

BABCOCK ROAD, SAN ANTONIO, UNITED STATES

WOODCOCK ROAD, ORLANDO, UNITED STATES

KITCHEN DICK ROAD, SEQUIM, UNITED STATES

BUMPASS ROAD, BUMPASS, UNITED STATES

BEAVER RUIN ROAD, NORCROSS, UNITED STATES

BIG BEAVER CREEK ROAD, SWANSEA, UNITED STATES

SHADES OF DEATH ROAD, WARREN, UNITED STATES

TOE JAM HILL ROAD, BAINBRIDGE ISLAND, UNITED STATES

WRONG WAY, CARY, UNITED STATES

PE'EPE'E WAY, HILO, UNITED STATES

MY WAY CIRCLE, WILMINGTON, UNITED STATES

SCULLY WAY, OTTAWA, CANADA

HALL WAY, HIGHLAND, UNITED STATES

SMOKEPIPE ROAD, SOUDERTON, UNITED STATES

OLD POSSUM HOLLER ROAD, HENDERSONVILLE, UNITED STATES

HAVITURE WAY, VALLEJO, UNITED STATES

MILKY WAY, VERONA, UNITED STATES

CRAB AND WINKLE WAY, CANTERBURY, ENGLAND

HARDMAN AVENUE, BREDBURY, ENGLAND

CRAPPS AVENUE, WEST COLUMBIA, UNITED STATES

COON HUNT COURT, COLUMBIA, UNITED STATES

GAYLORD PLACE, TAKANINI, NEW ZEALAND

DICK PLACE, NAPIER, NEW ZEALAND

FASCINATION PLACE, MILPITAS, UNITED STATES

ROMEO PLACE, FORTVILLE, UNITED STATES

CROTCH CRESCENT, OXFORD, ENGLAND

COCK BRIDGE, ABERDEENSHIRE, SCOTLAND

USELESS LOOP, WESTERN AUSTRALIA,
AUSTRALIA

JACKASS JUNCTION, OATMAN, UNITED STATES

2 AMERICAN SPOTS

CHICKEN, ALASKA

DEADHORSE, ALASKA

EEK, ALASKA

LEFTHAND BAY, ALASKA

NIGHTMUTE, ALASKA

UNALASKA, ALASKA

ARCADE, CALIFORNIA

AVOCADO, CALIFORNIA

BAGDAD, CALIFORNIA

BUMMERVILLE, CALIFORNIA

CLIPPER GAP, CALIFORNIA

CONFIDENCE, CALIFORNIA

COOL, CALIFORNIA

DATE CITY, CALIFORNIA

DEADWOOD, CALIFORNIA

DOG TOWN, CALIFORNIA

DUNMOVIN, CALIFORNIA

FAIR PLAY, CALIFORNIA

FORKS OF SALMON, CALIFORNIA

FORT DICK, CALIFORNIA

FREEDOM, CALIFORNIA

HALLELUJAH JUNCTION, CALIFORNIA

HARDY, CALIFORNIA

LAST CHANCE, CALIFORNIA

LITTLE PENNY, CALIFORNIA

MAD RIVER, CALIFORNIA

MYSTIC, CALIFORNIA

NEEDLES, CALIFORNIA

PEANUT, CALIFORNIA

PLASTER CITY, CALIFORNIA

RAGTOWN, CALIFORNIA

RAINBOW, CALIFORNIA

RELIEF, CALIFORNIA

RESCUE, CALIFORNIA

RICE, CALIFORNIA

ROUGH AND READY, CALIFORNIA

SCARFACE, CALIFORNIA

SECRET TOWN, CALIFORNIA

SOAPWEED, CALIFORNIA

SQUABBLETOWN, CALIFORNIA

STRAWBERRY, CALIFORNIA

SUCKER FLAT, CALIFORNIA

SURPRISE STATION, CALIFORNIA

TOADTOWN, CALIFORNIA

VOLCANO, CALIFORNIA

WEED, CALIFORNIA

WEEDPATCH, CALIFORNIA

WIMP, CALIFORNIA

YOU BET, CALIFORNIA

BEAVER, OREGON

BORING, OREGON

DRAIN, OREGON

IDIOTVILLE, OREGON

SODAVILLE, OREGON

ZIGZAG, OREGON

FORKS, WASHINGTON

GEORGE, WASHINGTON

HUMPTULIPS, WASHINGTON

INDEX, WASHINGTON

TUMWATER, WASHINGTON

WALLA WALLA, WASHINGTON

BELT, MONTANA

BIG ARM, MONTANA

BIGFORK, MONTANA

BIG SKY, MONTANA

CHECKERBOARD, MONTANA

DIVIDE, MONTANA

ELMO, MONTANA

EUREKA, MONTANA

HUNGRY HORSE, MONTANA

OPPORTUNITY, MONTANA

OUTLOOK, MONTANA

ROCKY BOY, MONTANA

SAINT REGIS, MONTANA

SQUARE BUTTE, MONTANA

SWEETGRASS, MONTANA

TWO DOT, MONTANA

YAAK, MONTANA

BAGGS, WYOMING

BIG SANDY, WYOMING

CAMEL HUMP, WYOMING

CHUGWATER, WYOMING

COKEVILLE, WYOMING

MEETEETSE, WYOMING

MUDDY GAP, WYOMING

POINT OF ROCKS, WYOMING

JACKPOT, NEVADA

SEARCHLIGHT, NEVADA

WEED HEIGHTS, NEVADA

BUNKERVILLE, NEVADA

CURRIE, NEVADA

DUCKWATER, NEVADA

PIOCHE, NEVADA

RACHEL, NEVADA

SMITH, NEVADA

HURRICANE, UTAH

MEXICAN HAT, UTAH

ORANGEVILLE, UTAH

ORDERVILLE, UTAH

PARADISE, UTAH

PLAIN, UTAH

CLIMAX, COLORADO

DINOSAUR, COLORADO

LAST CHANCE, COLORADO

NO NAME, COLORADO

PARACHUTE, COLORADO

SECURITY-WIDEFIELD, COLORADO

TINCUP, COLORADO

YELLOW JACKET, COLORADO

BUMBLE BEE, ARIZONA

CAREFREE, ARIZONA

CHLORIDE, ARIZONA

GOODYEAR, ARIZONA

MANY FARMS, ARIZONA

NOTHING, ARIZONA

SHOW LOW, ARIZONA

SURPRISE, ARIZONA

THREE FORKS, ARIZONA

TUBA CITY, ARIZONA

WHY, ARIZONA

WINKELMAN, ARIZONA

ELEPHANT BUTTE, NEW MEXICO

TEXICO, NEW MEXICO

TINGLE, NEW MEXICO

TRUTH OR CONSEQUENCES, NEW MEXICO

ANTLER, NORTH DAKOTA

COLGATE, NORTH DAKOTA

HOOPLE, NORTH DAKOTA

VOLTAIRE, NORTH DAKOTA

ZAP, NORTH DAKOTA

BLUE EARTH, MINNESOTA

CLIMAX, MINNESOTA

EMBARRASS, MINNESOTA

FERTILE, MINNESOTA

NIMROD, MINNESOTA

NOWTHEN, MINNESOTA

SAVAGE, MINNESOTA

SLEEPY EYE, MINNESOTA

BATH, SOUTH DAKOTA

EPIPHANY, SOUTH DAKOTA

FAITH, SOUTH DAKOTA

FARMER, SOUTH DAKOTA

GAYVILLE, SOUTH DAKOTA

GREEN GRASS, SOUTH DAKOTA

HAMMER, SOUTH DAKOTA

HITCHCOCK, SOUTH DAKOTA

IGLOO, SOUTH DAKOTA

JAVA, SOUTH DAKOTA

KIDDER, SOUTH DAKOTA

LEMMON, SOUTH DAKOTA

ORAL SOUTH DAKOTA

PARADE, SOUTH DAKOTA

PEEVER, SOUTH DAKOTA

POTATO CREEK, SOUTH DAKOTA

PRINGLE, SOUTH DAKOTA

PUMPKIN CENTER, SOUTH DAKOTA

RED SHIRT, SOUTH DAKOTA

TOLSTOY, SOUTH DAKOTA

VIENNA, SOUTH DAKOTA

WALL, SOUTH DAKOTA

WHITE, SOUTH DAKOTA

WOOD, SOUTH DAKOTA

YALE, SOUTH DAKOTA

DIAGONAL, IOWA

GRAVITY, IOWA

LOST NATION, IOWA

MANLY, IOWA

WHAT CHEER, IOWA

BEAVER CROSSING, NEBRASKA

COLON, NEBRASKA

FORT CROOK, NEBRASKA

LOUP CITY, NEBRASKA

SURPRISE, NEBRASKA

VALENTINE, NEBRASKA

WAHOO, NEBRASKA

WEEPING WATER, NEBRASKA

WORMS, NEBRASKA

ADMIRE, KANSAS

BUTTERMILK, KANSAS

CUBA, KANSAS

DENMARK, KANSAS

GAS, KANSAS

HOLLAND, KANSAS

RANSOM, KANSAS

ZURICH, KANSAS

BEAN LAKE STATION, MISSOURI

COLDWATER, MISSOURI

CONCEPTION, MISSOURI

ENOUGH, MISSOURI

FAIRDEALING, MISSOURI

FIDELITY, MISSOURI

FRANKENSTEIN, MISSOURI

HUMANSVILLE, MISSOURI

LICKING, MISSOURI

PARIS, MISSOURI

PECULIAR, MISSOURI

REFORM, MISSOURI

ROMANCE, MISSOURI

SLEEPER, MISSOURI

TIGHTWAD, MISSOURI

USEFUL, MISSOURI

BEETOWN, WISCONSIN

FOOTVILLE, WISCONSIN

IMALONE, WISCONSIN

SPREAD EAGLE, WISCONSIN

UBET, WISCONSIN

WANDEROOS, WISCONSIN

BAD AXE, MICHIGAN

CHRISTMAS, MICHIGAN

CLIMAX, MICHIGAN

EDEN, MICHIGAN

HELL, MICHIGAN

JUGVILLE, MICHIGAN

PIGEON, MICHIGAN

SLAPNECK, MICHIGAN

BIG FOOT PRAIRIE, ILLINOIS

FISHHOOK, ILLINOIS

GRAND DETOUR, ILLINOIS

KICKAPOO, ILLINOIS

NORMAL, ILLINOIS

PAW PAW, ILLINOIS

SANDWICH, ILLINOIS

ACME, INDIANA

BALLSTOWN, INDIANA

BEEHUNTER, INDIANA

CAREFREE, INDIANA

FICKLE, INDIANA

FLOYDS KNOBS, INDIANA

FRENCH LICK, INDIANA

GAS CITY, INDIANA

LOOGOOTEE, INDIANA

MUNSTER, INDIANA

SANTA CLAUS, INDIANA

SPRAYTOWN, INDIANA

TOAD HOP, INDIANA

BLUE BALL, OHIO

FLY, OHIO

HICKSVILLE, OHIO

KNOCKEMSTIFF, OHIO

TOBASCO, OHIO

3 GOOD OLD U.S.A.

MIANUS, CONNECTICUT

MOOSUP, CONNECTICUT

GAYLORDSVILLE, CONNECTICUT

QUONOCHONTAUG, RHODE ISLAND

WOONSOCKET, RHODE ISLAND

BELCHERTOWN, MASSACHUSETTS

BRAINTREE, MASSACHUSETTS

DOROTHY POND, MASSACHUSETTS

EGYPT, MASSACHUSETTS

GAY HEAD CLIFFS, MASSACHUSETTS

MARBLEHEAD, MASSACHUSETTS

MASHPEE, MASSACHUSETTS

NANTUCKET, MASSACHUSETTS

SWAMPSCOTT, MASSACHUSETTS

WARE, MASSACHUSETTS

BALD HEAD, MAINE

DICKEY, MAINE

BEAN'S PURCHASE, NEW HAMPSHIRE

BERLIN, NEW HAMPSHIRE

BOW, NEW HAMPSHIRE

CHESTERFIELD, NEW HAMPSHIRE

CONTOOCOOK, NEW HAMPSHIRE

OSSIPEE, NEW HAMPSHIRE

SANDWICH, NEW HAMPSHIRE

ROXBURY, NEW HAMPSHIRE

RYE, NEW HAMPSHIRE

SHARON, NEW HAMPSHIRE

MOSQUITOVILLE, VERMONT

JERICHO, VERMONT

SATAN'S KINGDOM, VERMONT

BALD KNOB, ARKANSAS

BIGGERS, ARKANSAS

CRAIGHEAD, ARKANSAS

FANNIE, ARKANSAS

FIFTY-SIX, ARKANSAS

GREASY CORNER, ARKANSAS

GRUBBS, ARKANSAS

HASTY, ARKANSAS

HOOKER, ARKANSAS

MAGAZINE, ARKANSAS

MOSCOW, ARKANSAS

NUCKLES, ARKANSAS

OKAY, ARKANSAS

POCAHONTAS, ARKANSAS

ROMANCE, ARKANSAS

SMACKOVER, ARKANSAS

TURKEY SCRATCH, ARKANSAS

UMPIRE, ARKANSAS

WEINER, ARKANSAS

BELCHER, LOUISIANA

BUNKIE, LOUISIANA

CONVENT, LOUISIANA

CUT OFF, LOUISIANA

DRY PRONG, LOUISIANA

EROS, LOUISIANA

FORT NECESSITY, LOUISIANA

GOODBEE, LOUISIANA

GROSSE TÊTE, LOUISIANA

JIGGER, LOUISIANA

MUDVILLE, LOUISIANA

INDEPENDENCE, LOUISIANA

WATERPROOF, LOUISIANA

BOWLEGS, OKLAHOMA

COOKIETOWN, OKLAHOMA

FROGVILLE, OKLAHOMA

HAPPYLAND, OKLAHOMA

HOOKER, OKLAHOMA

KREMLIN, OKLAHOMA

PUMPKIN CENTER, OKLAHOMA

SLAPOUT, OKLAHOMA

SLAUGHTERVILLE, OKLAHOMA

BEN HUR, TEXAS

BLACKJACK, TEXAS

CANADIAN, TEXAS

CHINA, TEXAS

COMFORT, TEXAS

CONVERSE, TEXAS

DING DONG, TEXAS

DIME BOX, TEXAS

EARTH, TEXAS

GUN BARREL CITY, TEXAS

HOOP AND HOLLER, TEXAS

LONDON, TEXAS

LOONEYVILLE, TEXAS

MULESHOE, TEXAS

OATMEAL, TEXAS

NOODLE, TEXAS

PAINT ROCK, TEXAS

PARIS, TEXAS

POINT BLANK, TEXAS

SMILEY, TEXAS

SUGAR LAND, TEXAS

TARZAN, TEXAS

TELEGRAPH, TEXAS

TELEPHONE, TEXAS

TROPHY CLUB, TEXAS

TURKEY, TEXAS

UNCERTAIN, TEXAS

VALENTINE, TEXAS

AIMWELL, ALABAMA

BURNT CORN, ALABAMA

ECLECTIC, ALABAMA

INTERCOURSE, ALABAMA

MUCK CITY, ALABAMA

BEAVERLICK, KENTUCKY

BUG, KENTUCKY

BUSY, KENTUCKY

BUTTERFLY, KENTUCKY

DO STOP, KENTUCKY

DRIP ROCK, KENTUCKY

DWARF, KENTUCKY

HI HAT, KENTUCKY

LICK FORK, KENTUCKY

MONKEY'S EYEBROW, KENTUCKY

OGLE, KENTUCKY

ORDINARY, KENTUCKY

RABBIT HASH, KENTUCKY

TYPO, KENTUCKY

UNO, KENTUCKY

ALLIGATOR, MISSISSIPPI

ARM, MISSISSIPPI

BOBO, MISSISSIPPI

BASIC, MISSISSIPPI

BATTLES, MISSISSIPPI

CHUNKY, MISSISSIPPI

COFFEEVILLE, MISSISSIPPI

DARLING, MISSISSIPPI

D'LO, MISSISSIPPI

DRAGON, MISSISSIPPI

EDEN, MISSISSIPPI

EGYPT, MISSISSIPPI

HOLLYWOOD, MISSISSIPPI

HOT COFFEE, MISSISSIPPI

KOKOMO, MISSISSIPPI

MIDNIGHT, MISSISSIPPI

SCOOBA, MISSISSIPPI

SOSO, MISSISSIPPI

TIE PLANT, MISSISSIPPI

WALLS, MISSISSIPPI

YAZOO CITY, MISSISSIPPI

BLUE GOOSE, TENNESSEE

BUGSCUFFLE, TENNESSEE

BUCKSNORT, TENNESSEE

DEFEATED, TENNESSEE

DIFFICULT, TENNESSEE

DISCO, TENNESSEE

DUCKTOWN, TENNESSEE

FINGER, TENNESSEE

ONLY, TENNESSEE

STATIC, TENNESSEE

SWEET LIPS, TENNESSEE

BLUE BALL, DELAWARE

COCKED HAT, DELAWARE

HOURGLASS, DELAWARE

LITTLE HEAVEN, DELAWARE

CHRISTMAS, FLORIDA

FROSTPROOF, FLORIDA

KISSIMMEE, FLORIDA

MAYO, FLORIDA

NICEVILLE, FLORIDA

RED HEAD, FLORIDA

SOPCHOPPY, FLORIDA

TWO EGG, FLORIDA

WEBSTER, FLORIDA

WEEKI WACHEE, FLORIDA

BETWEEN, GEORGIA

ENIGMA, GEORGIA

CUMMING, GEORGIA

HOPEULIKIT, GEORGIA

ROME, GEORGIA

SANTA CLAUS, GEORGIA

SNAPFINGER, GEORGIA

TALKING ROCK, GEORGIA

ACCIDENT, MARYLAND

ASSAWOMAN BAY, MARYLAND

CALIFORNIA, MARYLAND

COCKEYSVILLE, MARYLAND

POMONKEY, MARYLAND

SECRETARY, MARYLAND

AVON, NORTH CAROLINA

BAT CAVE, NORTH CAROLINA

BIG LICK, NORTH CAROLINA

BLOWING ROCK, NORTH CAROLINA

BOLIVIA, NORTH CAROLINA

DUCK, NORTH CAROLINA

GUM NECK, NORTH CAROLINA

HORNEYTOWN, NORTH CAROLINA

MEAT CAMP, NORTH CAROLINA

SPEED, NORTH CAROLINA

LITTLE SWITZERLAND, NORTH CAROLINA

TICK BITE, NORTH CAROLINA

TOAST, NORTH CAROLINA

WELCOME, NORTH CAROLINA

WHYNOT, NORTH CAROLINA

COWARD, SOUTH CAROLINA

DUE WEST, SOUTH CAROLINA

NINE TIMES, SOUTH CAROLINA

ROUND O, SOUTH CAROLINA

SOUTHERN SHOPS, SOUTH CAROLINA

SOUTH OF THE BORDER, SOUTH CAROLINA

ANTLERS, VIRGINIA

BAGDAD, VIRGINIA

CLAM, VIRGINIA

FRIES, VIRGINIA

GOOCHLAND, VIRGINIA

JAMAICA, VIRGINIA

JAVA, VIRGINIA

JOE NEETS, VIRGINIA

NEEDMORE, VIRGINIA

NUTTSVILLE, VIRGINIA

SHORT PUMP, VIRGINIA

SIMPLICITY, VIRGINIA

POCKET, VIRGINIA

BIG CHIMNEY, WEST VIRGINIA

BIG UGLY, WEST VIRGINIA

CRUM, WEST VIRGINIA

FIVEMILE, WEST VIRGINIA

FRIENDLY, WEST VIRGINIA

HOOHOO, WEST VIRGINIA

HUNDRED, WEST VIRGINIA

KERMIT, WEST VIRGINIA

MAN, WEST VIRGINIA

PAW PAW, WEST VIRGINIA

PINCH, WEST VIRGINIA

QUICK, WEST VIRGINIA

WAR, WEST VIRGINIA

4 OH' CANADA

ALICE ARM, BRITISH COLUMBIA

BALDY HUGHES, BRITISH COLUMBIA

BLIND CHANNEL, BRITISH COLUMBIA

BLISS LANDING, BRITISH COLUMBIA

BLUBBER BAY, BRITISH COLUMBIA

BURNT FLAT, BRITISH COLUMBIA

CHASE, BRITISH COLUMBIA

DOG CREEK, BRITISH COLUMBIA

FALSE BAY, BRITISH COLUMBIA

GANG RANCH, BRITISH COLUMBIA

HORSEFLY, BRITISH COLUMBIA

HYDRAULIC, BRITISH COLUMBIA

KAMLOOPS, BRITISH COLUMBIA

MOOSE HEIGHTS, BRITISH COLUMBIA

PENNY, BRITISH COLUMBIA

SALMON ARM, BRITISH COLUMBIA

SKOOKUMCHUCK, BRITISH COLUMBIA

SODA CREEK, BRITISH COLUMBIA

SPUZZUM, BRITISH COLUMBIA

STONER, BRITISH COLUMBIA

TA TA CREEK, BRITISH COLUMBIA

BEARBERRY, ALBERTA

BEAVER CROSSING, ALBERTA

BIG STONE, ALBERTA

BUFFALO HEAD PRAIRIE, ALBERTA

CARROT CREEK, ALBERTA

CZAR, ALBERTA

FLYINGSHOT LAKE, ALBERTA

GOODFISH LAKE, ALBERTA

KEG RIVER, ALBERTA

LITTLE SMOKY, ALBERTA

MEDICINE HAT, ALBERTA

MILK RIVER, ALBERTA

MIRROR, ALBERTA

NOJACK, ALBERTA

ROCKY MOUNTAIN HOUSE, ALBERTA

SEVEN PERSONS, ALBERTA

STAND OFF, ALBERTA

VULCAN, ALBERTA

WANDERING RIVER, ALBERTA

WESTWARD HO, ALBERTA

WHISKEY GAP, ALBERTA

WILD HORSE, ALBERTA

WOOD BUFFALO, ALBERTA

BIGGAR, SASKATCHEWAN

CADILLAC, SASKATCHEWAN

CUT KNIFE, SASKATCHEWAN

DRINKWATER, SASKATCHEWAN

ELBOW, SASKATCHEWAN

CORNY NAMES & STUPID PLACES

EYEBROW, SASKATCHEWAN

FAIRY GLEN, SASKATCHEWAN

FERTILE, SASKATCHEWAN

GRANDMOTHER'S BAY, SASKATCHEWAN

HOLDFAST, SASKATCHEWAN

MOOSE JAW, SASKATCHEWAN

NUT MOUNTAIN, SASKATCHEWAN

OLD WIVES, SASKATCHEWAN

PRIMATE, SASKATCHEWAN

SANCTUARY, SASKATCHEWAN

SMUTS, SASKATCHEWAN

SPY HILL, SASKATCHEWAN

SUCCESS, SASKATCHEWAN

SUCKER RIVER, SASKATCHEWAN

URANIUM CITY, SASKATCHEWAN

BACON RIDGE, MANITOBA

BIRDTAIL, MANITOBA

CAMPER, MANITOBA

DROPMORE, MANITOBA

FINGER, MANITOBA

FLIN FLON, MANITOBA

JACKHEAD, MANITOBA

MOOSEHORN, MANITOBA

SNOWFLAKE, MANITOBA

STARBUCK, MANITOBA

VIVIAN, MANITOBA

WHITE MUD FALLS, MANITOBA

WINDYGATES, MANITOBA

AZILDA, ONTARIO

BENT RIVER, ONTARIO

BIG CHUTE, ONTARIO

BRIGHT, ONTARIO

BUMMERS´ ROOST, ONTARIO

BUZWAH, ONTARIO

CAPE CROKER, ONTARIO

CARRYING PLACE, ONTARIO

CHEAPSIDE, ONTARIO

EDEN, ONTARIO

HOARDS, ONTARIO

NEW CREDIT, ONTARIO

PAIN COURT, ONTARIO

PICKLE LAKE, ONTARIO

PRECIOUS CORNERS, ONTARIO

PROTON STATION, ONTARIO

SHINING TREE, ONTARIO

SILVER DOLLAR, ONTARIO

SNOWBALL, ONTARIO

SNUG HARBOUR, ONTARIO

SOUR SPRING, ONTARIO

SWORDS, ONTARIO

TINY, ONTARIO

UPHILL, ONTARIO

WAWA, ONTARIO

WHITEDOG, ONTARIO

WILD GOOSE, ONTARIO

WISEMAN'S CORNERS, ONTARIO

5 HEY CANADA

ASBESTOS, QUEBEC

CADILLAC, QUEBEC

CAP-CHAT, QUEBEC

CHANDLER, QUEBEC

CHAPEAU, QUEBEC

CRABTREE, QUEBEC

DUNDEE, QUEBEC

OLD FACTORY, QUEBEC

LÉVIS, QUEBEC

MAYO, QUEBEC

PRICE, QUEBEC

SAINT-LOUIS-DU-HA! HA! QUEBEC

BURNT CHURCH, NEW BRUNSWICK

CARLETON, NEW BRUNSWICK

CHANCE HARBOUR, NEW BRUNSWICK

MOUNTAIN PLEASANT CALDERA, NEW BRUNSWICK

PLASTER ROCK, NEW BRUNSWICK

POKEMOUCHE, NEW BRUNSWICK

STANLEY, NEW BRUNSWICK

SUNNY CORNER, NEW BRUNSWICK

WOOD POINT, NEW BRUNSWICK

CHARLOTTETOWN, PRINCE EDWARD ISLAND

CRAPAUD, PRINCE EDWARD ISLAND

POINT PRIM, PRINCE EDWARD ISLAND

SAVAGE HARBOUR, PRINCE EDWARD ISLAND

SKINNER'S POND, PRINCE EDWARD ISLAND

BIBLE HILL, NOVA SCOTIA

BUCKLAW, NOVA SCOTIA

CONCESSION, NOVA SCOTIA

COXHEATH, NOVA SCOTIA

CROW'S NEST, NOVA SCOTIA

CORNY NAMES & STUPID PLACES

ECUM SECUM, NOVA SCOTIA

EGYPT ROAD, NOVA SCOTIA

GARDEN OF EDEN, NOVA SCOTIA

LAND OF LAZINESS LAKE, NOVA SCOTIA

LOWER ECONOMY, NOVA SCOTIA

MIRA GUT, NOVA SCOTIA

MUSHABOOM, NOVA SCOTIA

PLEASANTVILLE, NOVA SCOTIA

ROACHVALE, NOVA SCOTIA

HEAD OF ST. MARGARETS BAY, NOVA SCOTIA

SHAG HARBOUR, NOVA SCOTIA

SOBER ISLAND, NOVA SCOTIA

YANKEETOWN, NOVA SCOTIA

ENTERPRISE, NORTHWEST TERRITORIES

FORT RESOLUTION, NORTHWEST TERRITORIES

PRINCE PATRICK, NORTHWEST TERRITORIES

WEKWETI, NORTHWEST TERRITORIES

YELLOWKNIFE, NORTHWEST TERRITORIES

BROOKS BROOK, YUKON TERRITORY

CHAMPAGNE, YUKON TERRITORY

KENO CITY, YUKON TERRITORY

PARIS, YUKON TERRITORY

SIXTY MILE, YUKON TERRITORY

SNAG, YUKON TERRITORY

WHITEHORSE, YUKON TERRITORY

6 STRANGE WORLD

BATMAN, TURKEY

DEAD CHINAMAN, PAPUA GUINEA

DONGO, CONGO

DUM DUM, INDIA

DUMDUMI, INDIA

FUKA, NIGERIA

HELL, CAYMAN ISLANDS

HOMO, PERU

LITTLE DIX, ANGUILLA

MONKEY TOWN, TRINIDAD AND TOBAGO

OUAGADOUGOU, BURKINA FASO

SEXY, PERU

SEYMEN, TURKEY

SHIT, IRAN

SHITKA, RUSSIA

TURDY, TAJIKISTAN

WANKIE (NAME CHANGED TO HWANGE),
ZIMBABWE

AGAY, FRANCE

BORING, DENAMARK

BITCHE, FRANCE

BREST, FRANCE

BYE, JÄMTLAND, SWEDEN

CONDOM, FRANCE

CORNY, FRANCE

LES GETS, FRANCE

LOL, DORDOGNE, FRANCE

MISERY, PICARDIE, FRANCE

MOLDE, NORWAY

NOKIA, FINLAND

PISSY, FRANCE

SLUT, SWEDEN

SEXBIERUM, NETHERLANDS

LE TAMPON, FRANCE

ASS, UKRAINE

BOLOGNA, ITALY

CLIT RIVER, ROMANIA

CUNTER, SWITZERLAND

FUCKING, AUSTRIA

GRANADA, SPAIN

LAZIO, ITALY

LESBOS ISLAND, GREECE

LOO, ESTONTIA

PEÑÍSCOLA, SPAIN

PILES, SPAIN

PÜSSI, ESTONIA

MOUNT TITLIS, SWITZERLAND

TURDA, ROMANIA

7 SAUCY PLACES

BAD KISSINGEN, GERMANY

FOCKENDORF, GERMANY

ITZEHOE, GERMANY

KISSING, GERMANY

PETTING, GERMANY

PISSEN, GERMANY

RIMSTING, GERMANY

RÖCKEN, GERMANY

SPIELBERG, GERMANY

TITTING, GERMANY

TITZ, GERMANY

WANK, GERMANY

WANKENDORF, GERMANY

WANKUM, GERMANY

WORMS, GERMANY

BANGKOK, THAILAND

FUKUYAMA, JAPAN

FUKUE ISLAND, JAPAN

GAYAMAN, PHILIPPINES

KUNT'ONG-DONG, NORTH KOREA

PING RIVER, THAILAND

SEXMOAN (NAME CHANGED TO SASMUAN), PHILIPPINES

TAKESHITA STREET, JAPAN

TE PUKE, NEW ZEALAND

TONG FUK, HONG KONG

WAIPU, NEW ZEALAND

WHAKAPAPA VILLAGE, NEW ZEALAND

WHAKATANE, NEW ZEALAND

BALD KNOB, AUSTRALIA

BOBS FARM, AUSTRALIA

BENJABERRING, AUSTRALIA

BEERMULLAH, AUSTRALIA

BOBBIN HEAD, AUSTRALIA

KIAMA BLOWHOLE, AUSTRALIA

BRAIDWOOD, AUSTRALIA

BROKEN HILL, AUSTRALIA

CHRISTMAS CREEK MINE, AUSTRALIA

CHRISTMAS ISLAND, AUSTRALIA

COCKBURN, AUSTRALIA

DELICATE NOBBY, AUSTRALIA

DUNDEE, AUSTRALIA

EGGS & BACON BAY, AUSTRALIA

FAIRYMEAD, AUSTRALIA

GEELONG, AUSTRALIA

GUYS FOREST, AUSTRALIA

HAT HEAD, AUSTRALIA

HOWLONG, AUSTRALIA

INNALOO, AUSTRALIA

IPSWICH, AUSTRALIA

JIMBOOMBA, AUSTRALIA

MOOBALL, AUSTRALIA

NEVERTIRE, AUSTRALIA

NOWHERE ELSE, AUSTRALIA

PORT FAIRY, AUSTRALIA

SAFETY BAY, AUSTRALIA

THE ROCK, AUSTRALIA

TITTYBONG, AUSTRALIA

WAGGA, WAGGA, AUSTRALIA

WANGI, WANGI, AUSTRALIA

WARDS MISTAKE, AUSTRALIA

WATANOBBI, AUSTRALIA

WEE WAA, AUSTRALIA

8 BRITAIN ROCKS!

DUMFRIES AND GALLOWAY, SCOTLAND

BACKSIDE, SCOTLAND

BADCALL, SCOTLAND

BOGHEAD, SCOTLAND

BOYSACK, SCOTLAND

BURN OF ALLANSTANK, SCOTLAND

BUTT OF LEWIS, SCOTLAND

DUNBOG, SCOTLAND

HOLLYBUSH, SCOTLAND

INCHBARE, SCOTLAND

KNOCKGLASS, SCOTLAND

MEIKLE TARTY, SCOTLAND

TWATT, SCOTLAND

BARKING, ENGLAND

BRAINTREE, ENGLAND

BUMBLE'S GREEN, ENGLAND

BUTT'S GREEN, ENGLAND

COGGESGALL, ENGLAND

DUCK END, ENGLAND

FINGRINGHOE, ENGLAND

FIDDLERS HAMLET, ENGLAND

FOULNESS ISLAND, ENGLAND

GREAT SALING, ENGLAND

HIGH EASTER, ENGLAND

KIRBY-LE-SOKEN, ENGLAND

MESSING-CUM-INWORTH, ENGLAND

ROTTEN END, ENGLAND

SEVEN KINGS, ENGLAND

TOOT HILL, ENGLAND

UGLEY, ENGLAND

YOUNG'S END, ENGLAND

BACHELOR'S BUMP, ENGLAND

BEGGARS BUSH, ENGLAND

BLACKBOYS, ENGLAND

BURNT OAK, ENGLAND

COWBEECH, ENGLAND

GORING-BY-SEA, ENGLAND

GUN HILL, ENGLAND

HOOE, ENGLAND

MUDDLES GREEN, ENGLAND

COMPTON, ENGLAND

CRABTREE, ENGLAND

LICKFOLD, ENGLAND

NUTHURST, ENGLAND

MANNINGS HEATH, ENGLAND

MONK'S GATE, ENGLAND

RIPE, ENGLAND

UPPER BEEDING, ENGLAND

UPPER DICKER, ENGLAND

WOODEND, ENGLAND

BROWN WILLY, ENGLAND

COCKS, ENGLAND

HERODSFOOT, ENGLAND

JOLLY'S BOTTOM, ENGLAND

MOUSEHOLE, ENGLAND

POLYPHANT, ENGLAND

TITSON, ENGLAND

TWELVEHEADS, ENGLAND

WASHAWAY, ENGLAND

SCRATCHY BOTTOM, ENGLAND

HAPPY BOTTOM, ENGLAND

SHAGGS, ENGLAND

SHITTERTON, ENGLAND

POKESDOWN, ENGLAND

PUDDLETOWN, ENGLAND

WATCHET, ENGLAND

SIMONSBATH, ENGLAND

CATSGORE, ENGLAND

BEDBURN, ENGLAND

BURNT HOUSES, ENGLAND

PITY ME, ENGLAND

SOCKBURN, ENGLAND

WATERHOUSES, ENGLAND

APES HALL, ENGLAND

LITTLE WRATTING, ENGLAND

MUCH HADHAM, ENGLAND

PIDLEY, ENGLAND

SIX MILE BOTTOM, ENGLAND

STEEPLE BUMPSTEAD, ENGLAND

TICK FEN, ENGLAND

WARBOYS, ENGLAND

WENDY, ENGLAND

BREACH, ENGLAND

HAM, ENGLAND

SANDWICH, ENGLAND

GRAVESEND, ENGLAND

LOOSE, ENGLAND

MOCKBEGGAR, ENGLAND

TOY'S HILL, ENGLAND

THONG, ENGLAND

9 BRITISH SPOTS

CALIFORNIA, ENGLAND

CASTLE RISING, ENGLAND

DAMGATE, ENGLAND

FAKENHAM, ENGLAND

GREAT SNORING, ENGLAND

HORSEY, ENGLAND

KENNY HILL, ENGLAND

LIMPENHOE, ENGLAND

LITTLE SNORING, ENGLAND

POTT ROW, ENGLAND

PUDDLEDOCK, ENGLAND

STIFFKEY, ENGLAND

TITCHWELL, ENGLAND

BLOODY BRIDGE, IRELAND

BURNFOOT, IRELAND

CAMP, IRELAND

COOKSTOWN, IRELAND

CROOKSTOWN, IRELAND

DOOMORE, IRELAND

EFFIN, IRELAND

GAY TOWN, IRELAND

HACKBALLSCROSS, IRELAND

INCH, IRELAND

KILL, IRELAND

KILKENNY, IRELAND

KILBRITTAIN, IRELAND

MUFF, IRELAND

NEW TWOPOTHOUSE, IRELAND

NOBBER, IRELAND

OVENS, IRELAND

QUILTY, IRELAND

TANG, IRELAND

TERMONFECKIN, IRELAND

BLUE BALL, IRELAND

TRIM, IRELAND

WINDGAP, IRELAND

BANGOR, WALES

BLACKWOOD, WALES

BRITON FERRY, WALES

BULLY HOLE BOTTOM, WALES

FISHGUARD, WALES

HAY-ON-WYE, WALES

HOLYHEAD, WALES

LITTLE MOUNTAIN, WALES

MOLD, FLINTSHIRE, WALES

SODOM, FLINTSHIRE, WALES

STOP-AND-CALL, WALES

TARTS HILL, WALES

THREE COCKS, WALES

BLACK DOG, ENGLAND

CLAPWORTHY, ENGLAND

COCK HILL, ENGLAND

COFFINSWELL, ENGLAND

CRACKPOT, ENGLAND

DOG VILLAGE, ENGLAND

FELLDOWNHEAD, ENGLAND

FOLLY GATE, ENGLAND

GIGGLESWICK, ENGLAND

HINDERWELL, ENGLAND

HOLE BOTTOM, ENGLAND

HORWOOD, ENGLAND

JUMP, ENGLAND

KNOTTY CORNER, ENGLAND

LAND OF NOD, ENGLAND

PENNYCOMEQUICK, ENGLAND

SEXHOW, ENGLAND

WETWANG, ENGLAND

10 CORNY NAMES

BARB DWYER

HARRY PITTS

CHRIS P. BACON

CLAIRE ANNETTE

DICK BURNS

DON KEY

ESTELLE HURTZ

JACK HAAS

JUSTIN CASE

RICH GUY

LON MOORE

LES PAYNE

KAY BULL

LAURA NORDER

WANDA RIN

PHIL GRAVES

MINNIE BARR

ROBIN BANKS

RAY DEO

GAYE BARR

BOB KATZ

IZZY CUMMING

CHEW KOK

YU WINN

DAN SINGH

KULBIR MANN

PHAT HO

SUKHDEEP

RAMANDEEP

CHEE TIN HO

HU FLUNG PU

CY NARRA

LONG WANG

HUNG LO

YURI SLUTSKY

SUE YU

SUE SHEE

IMAN S. HOLE

PEE DON YU

SUM DUM GAI

SUM YUNG HO

TAI MI SHU

WEI WONG

WONG TERN

YUNG N. DOM

MR. AZHUL

PHIL LANG

OLIVE YEW

BILL DING

SUM POON TANG

MAJOR HARDON

PRIVATE PARTZ

ART MAJOR

DR. LOONEY

DR.LES PLACK

DR. JUSTIN PAYNE

DR. WHITEHEAD

DR. RASH

DR. PEPPER

DR. MOLLAR

DR. KWAK

DR. HART

DR. CHU

DR. FANG

DR. HURT

DR. NUTT

DR.WIENER

DR. GUTMAN

DR. LOVE

SANDY BUSH

OLIVE GREEN

EARL E. HARDON

PAIGE TURNER

PEPE RONI

TAD MOORE

MIKE WIENER

PHIL LANG

LES STROKER

DICK HEAD

DARYL RHEA

MILLY GRAHM

ANITA HOOKER

TAD MOORE

DICK FRYER

RAY PIST

ZACK LEE WRIGHT

AL BEBACK

JAY WALKER

JEAN POOLE

WOODY FORREST

HARRY BEAVER

WOODY FONDLER

HARRY COX

ANITA MANDALAY

RICH HOOKER

MIKE HUNT

EATON BUSH

JACK GOFF

PAT HISCOCK

WANDA SWALLOW

DICK COLON

SHARON PARTNERS

PIERCE COX

DICK HYMAN

MONA LOTT

HARRY KUNTZ

HARRY WANG

DICK HERTZ

ANITA HOARE

WILLIE STROKER

DICK FAYCE

JOE KING

MANNY KIN

TIM BURR

VAL LAY

EATON WRIGHT

DOUG GRAVES

MAX POWER

PAT BUTT

SID DOWNE

TED E. BAER

WAYNE DEER

AL BINO

BEN DOVER

BUZZ ZING

FRANK N. STEIN

HARRY COX

JOE KERR

SUE FLAY

RHEA CURRAN

YORA HOGG

WOODY DEWITT

AL CAHAL

HOLLY WOOD

CORNY NAMES & STUPID PLACES

KAY NYNE

ANITA BATH

BOBBY PYN

KERRY OAKEY

WILLIE DEWER

SONNY DAY

TOM KATT

POLLY ESTHER

NEIL DOWNE

ANITA PHILIP

SKIP ROPER

TOMMY JEAN

WAYNE KING

LOU POOLE

WILLY WAITE

IONA FORD

WILL POWER

SUE CASE

EARL YEE

BUCK NOOD

CARL ARM

STAN DOWNE

WILLIE B. LONG

RAY BEEZE

MAX E. PADD

LOU ZAR

MARTY GRAW

CANDY GRAHM

JIM SCHWARTZ

IVAN ORDER

ANITA NEWMAN

STU PITT

CLAY TORRES

BEA MERRY

DWAYNE PIPE

CHRIS KROSS

ANITA HANDCOCK

DUSTY RHODES

LEE KING

DICK DAILY

BEA MANN

CANDI KANE

PETE MOSS

ANITA BLACKMAN

AMANDA LAY

PARKER CARR

HARRY PALMER

BO NOR

PAUL BEARER

JACK HAMMER

MEL ESTHER

ANNE TEAK

MARK KERR

DICK LES

BILL LONEY

TISH HUGHES

JOY RIDER

KENNY DEWITT

SHARON HEAD

OLIVER BUSH

EILEEN ULICK

MARY JOHANNA

ANITA WOODY

MYLES LONG

NOAH PEELE

OMAR GOSH

DIXON COCKS

BUSTER HYMEN

RAM DASS

PHIL McCRAKEN

PHYLIS STEIN

CY PHYLLIS

STAN DAUP

WILL BARROW

ANITA DYCK

ABOUT THE AUTHOR

Sidney S. Prasad is an author who is on the quest to make the world laugh. His work is focused on entertaining people with his dry humored novels. Sidney S. Prasad personally believes laughter is the best cure for all of life's ups and downs. Some other humorous books written by Sidney S. Prasad include: How To Piss Off A Telemarketer, Don't Ask Dumb Questions!, My Bipolar Manager, Misfortune Cookies, Plenty Of Freaks: Are You Sold On Online Dating? and Telemarketer's Revenge: The Customer Is Always Wrong, Bitch!

www.ingramcontent.com/pod-product-compliance
Lightning Source LLC
Chambersburg PA
CBHW071625040426
42452CB00009B/1483